SCHIZOID PER

DISORDER

Navigating Isolation and Embracing Individuality

DR. EMILY WATSON

CONTENTS

CHAPTER 1

Introduction to Schizoid Personality Disorder

SPD Definition

The mental health disease known as schizoid personality disorder (SPD) is characterized by a recurring pattern of social withdrawal and a constrained range of emotional expression. People with SPD frequently prefer solitude and struggle to establish and sustain meaningful interpersonal relationships. They frequently exhibit introspection, emotional distance, and a disinterest in societal mores and customs. The ability to participate in and take pleasure in social interactions, romantic relationships, and other parts of daily life can all be adversely impacted by this illness. The Diagnostic and Statistical Manual of Mental Disorders, Fifth Edition (DSM-5) lists it as one of the personality disorders.

Historical Background and Identification

Schizoid Personality Disorder (SPD) in Historical Context and Diagnosis:

The history of schizoid personality disorder is complicated, and over time, there have been many shifts in how it is recognized and understood. Here is a quick summary:

1. Initial Observations Early psychoanalytic theorists like Sigmund Freud introduced the idea of schizoid features when he referred to some people as having a "schizoid disposition." However, greater formal acknowledgement and research into this personality style didn't start until the middle of the 20th century.

Classification by DSM: In its second edition (DSM-II), which was released in 1968, the Diagnostic and Statistical Manual of Mental Disorders (DSM) for the first time recognized Schizoid Personality Disorder. It was characterized by a propensity for a solitary existence and a lack of interest in or appreciation of interpersonal relationships.

Changing Definitions

The SPD criteria were improved in later DSM editions (DSM-III, DSM-IV, and DSM-5). These changes seek to improve the diagnostic precision and set SPD apart from similar personality disorders like Schizotypal Personality Disorder and Avoidant Personality Disorder.

4. Recognition Obstacles: In both clinical practice and research, SPD has frequently been overshadowed by other personality disorders. Its mild and less obvious symptoms, as well as its similarities to other illnesses, have made recognition and diagnosis difficult.

5. Research and Awareness: There has been an increase in interest in comprehending SPD better in recent years. In order to understand its intricacies, researchers have looked into its genetic, neurological, and psychological foundations.

6. Treatment Focus: Since SPD has been recognized, therapy modalities have been created that are specifically geared toward addressing the difficulties SPD sufferers confront. With the use of these methods, people can enhance their quality of life and cultivate stronger interpersonal relationships.

Prevalence and Misperceptions

Misperceptions about Schizoid Personality Disorder (SPD) and its Prevalence:

Prevalence:

1. Low Prevalence: One of the less frequent personality disorders is SPD. Less than 1% of the general population is thought to be affected, though prevalence numbers can vary.

2. Gender Differences: Although some studies indicate that men may be more likely than women to have SPD, this gender difference is not always evident.

Misconceptions:

1. Confusion with Schizophrenia: One widespread misunderstanding is that SPD and schizophrenia are the same thing. These are separate illnesses. While both SPD and schizophrenia are classified as "schizoid," SPD is characterized by social and emotional withdrawal, whereas schizophrenia is marked by hallucinations, delusions, and significant disruptions in perception and thought.

2. Misunderstanding Emotional Expression: It's important to understand that people with SPD do experience feelings, despite the perception that they are emotionally numb or distant. They frequently struggle to communicate their sentiments in normal ways.

3. Introversion vs. SPD: A desire for solitude or introversion is not the same as SPD. Many introverts enjoy being around people, but they also want alone to

refuel. A chronic and excessive avoidance of intimate relationships is a feature of SPD.

4. Lack of Relationship Desire: It's a myth that people with SPD don't want to be in relationships. Even while they may seek relationships, they may find it difficult to maintain them on an emotional and social level.

5. Incurable or Untreatable: Another myth is that SPD is incurable and cannot be treated. Therapy and support can assist people with SPD in improving their social functioning and quality of life, even though it can be difficult to cure.

6. Stigmatization: Because of the myths and misunderstandings surrounding SPD, those who have the condition may experience stigma or prejudice, which makes it even harder for them to get support and assistance.

Promoting empathy, early intervention, and successful treatment for people with this personality disorder depends on recognizing the true nature of SPD and debunking these myths.

CHAPTER 2

Schizoid People's Private Lives

Internal Perspective on SPD

From the Inside: Understanding Schizoid Personality Disorder (SPD)

1. Emotional Detachment: One of the distinguishing traits of SPD sufferers is emotional detachment. They frequently feel feelings yet find it difficult to communicate them verbally or emotionally with others. This distance can cause a feeling of loneliness and make it challenging to build strong relationships.

2. desire for isolation: SPD sufferers frequently have a strong desire for isolation and may find comfort in solitary pursuits like reading, hobbies, or reflection. This withdrawal from social interaction is a coping mechanism, not necessarily a rejection of others.

3. Small Social Circle: If they have a social circle at all, it is usually limited to a few close friends and family members. It might be overwhelming or unfulfilling to maintain connections or partake in social activities.

4. Difficulty Expressing Feelings: People with SPD may find it difficult to vocally or through non-verbal clues express their feelings. They could find it difficult to express their happiness, grief, or rage in a way that others can understand.

5. Conflict Avoidance: They seek to avoid conflict and may take extraordinary measures to keep emotional distance from others in circumstances that could result in disagreement or conflict.

6. Heightened Self-Reliance: People with SPD frequently place a high value on independence and self-sufficiency. They might feel at ease in their own company and do well in jobs that call for independence.

7. Creative and Intellectual Activities: Many SPD sufferers have vibrant inner lives and may be excellent at creative or intellectual activities. They frequently find comfort and satisfaction in pursuits that provide them the freedom to express themselves without the constraints of social interaction.

8. Seeking Acceptance and Understanding: People with SPD may yearn for acceptance and understanding from others despite their social difficulties. They could value relationships that provide them a place to be themselves that is safe and judgment-free.

Common Characteristics and Traits

Schizoid Personality Disorder (SPD) Common Traits and Characteristics

1. Emotional Distancing: People with SPD frequently have a widespread pattern of emotional distancing. They could struggle to communicate their feelings to others and may find it difficult to relate to them emotionally.

2. Limited Social Interest: People with SPD typically show less interest in establishing and sustaining intimate bonds with others. They can favor solitary pursuits and seclusion over social connection.

3. Limited Expression: Their emotional expression may be constrained and come across as flat or subdued to others. Even in circumstances that generally arouse intense emotions, they might not express the entire spectrum of emotions that most people do.

4. Solitary Lifestyle: People with SPD frequently lead solitary lives. They may select occupations or pastimes that allow for independence, or they may partake in pursuits that don't necessitate frequent social connection.

5. Few Close Relationships: People with SPD often have very few, if any, close and intimate relationships, despite the possibility of acquaintances. They could have trouble building strong relationships with others.

6. Preference for Intellectual Activities: A lot of SPD sufferers have a keen interest in intellectual or artistic activities. They might flourish in occupations that need substantial thought and little interaction with others.

7. Aversion to Small Talk: People with SPD may find lighthearted conversation and casual social encounters awkward or boring. They could find it difficult to participate in talks that lack a defined goal or interesting topics.

8. Avoidance of Intimacy: They frequently steer clear of circumstances or connections that demand a lot of emotional intimacy. The avoidance of certain issues might make romantic relationships difficult.

9. Difficulty Making and Keeping Friends: People with SPD may find it challenging to make and keep friends. They might not actively seek out social interactions, and others may find it difficult to relate to them because of their lack of emotional expressiveness.

10. Indifference to Praise or Criticism: People with SPD may come across as unconcerned with both positive and constructive criticism. They might not look to others for affirmation or acceptance in the same way that many individuals do.

While these symptoms and characteristics are typical of SPD, it's crucial to remember that each person will experience the illness differently. A skilled mental health expert should diagnose someone after carefully examining their behavior and symptoms.

Emotional Experience and Coping Mechanisms

Emotional Experience and Coping Strategies in Schizoid Personality Disorder (SPD):

1. Emotional Suppression: People with SPD may use emotional suppression as a coping method. To preserve their preferred emotional detachment, they may intentionally or unconsciously repress their emotions.

2. Intellectualization: As a means of handling their emotions, they frequently rely on intellectualization. They could analyze and reason their emotions instead of expressing them in a traditional emotional way, keeping them at a cognitive distance.

3. Alone Time: Hobbies or other pursuits that need solitude are frequently used as coping mechanisms. These pursuits offer emotional control and a sense of pleasure without the necessity for social interaction.

4. Avoidance of Emotionally Stimulating Situations: People with SPD may purposefully steer clear of emotionally upsetting circumstances or people. They do this to lessen discomfort and preserve emotional stability.

5. Selective Emotional Engagement: Some SPD sufferers may only communicate their emotions to a small group of close friends while keeping emotional distance from the majority of others.

6. confrontation Avoidance: People with SPD may find it difficult to deal with confrontation. To avoid emotional turbulence, they frequently steer clear of disputes and altercations.

7. Emotional Numbing: People with SPD may utilize substances or participate in actions that temporarily dull their feelings. This may ease the discomfort that comes with having intense emotions.

8. Self-Reliance: They frequently place a high value on independence and may choose to manage emotional difficulties on their own. It could be thought of as a show of vulnerability to ask for assistance or support from others.

9. Minimal Social Engagement: One of the main symptoms of SPD is difficulty navigating social interactions. They might avoid situations or groups that would call for emotional participation, or they might keep social engagements to a minimum.

10. Longing for Connection: Despite their coping strategies, people with SPD may harbor a strong desire for empathy and understanding. It can be upsetting to feel this internal tension between a person's need for connection and their emotional distance.

CHAPTER 3

Diagnosis and evaluation

Finding SPD: Symptoms and Signs

Schizoid Personality Disorder (SPD) Signs and Symptoms: Identification

A pattern of behavior and personality characteristics that appear over time define schizoid personality disorder. While it's crucial to speak with a mental health expert for a correct diagnosis, the following are typical SPD symptoms and signs:

1. Emotional Detachment: People with SPD frequently struggle to articulate their emotions and come out as emotionally cold. They might appear unconcerned or unaffected by circumstances that ordinarily cause others to react emotionally strongly.

2. Limited Social Relationships: They tend to have few if any, close friends or personal relationships and a clear

preference for isolation. Social encounters tend to be scarce and might sometimes feel forced or uneasy.

3. Indifference to Accolades or Criticism: People with SPD may have an indifferent response to both positive and constructive criticism. They might not look for affirmation or praise, and they might not be adversely affected by criticism.

4. Preference for Alone Activities: They frequently participate in hobbies or work that permits them to be alone for long periods. These pursuits provide people with a sense of fulfillment and comfort.

5. Relationship Initiation Challenges: Establishing new connections, particularly romantic ones, can be difficult. They might not have the drive or desire to start and maintain social interactions.

6. Their ability to express their emotions fully is frequently limited. They could come out as somber,

making few motions and facial expressions. They could come out as distant or aloof to others.

7. Lack of Close Confidants: People with SPD typically do not have many close friends or family members with whom they may confide and express their feelings. They frequently conceal their innermost feelings.

8. imagination preoccupation: Some people may have elaborate daydreams or rich inner imagination worlds that take the place of emotional and social interaction.

9. Avoiding Small Talk: People with SPD may find it difficult to engage in casual social interactions and steer clear of settings involving brief exchanges of information.

10. Although it's not a universal characteristic, many SPD sufferers may have little interest in or experience with sexual interactions.

It's crucial to keep in mind that a mental health specialist should evaluate these signs and symptoms to see if they are consistent with SPD or another disease. Additionally, the intensity of SPD can vary, and not everyone who has it will experience all of its symptoms. To make an accurate diagnosis and consider the best course of therapy, a thorough evaluation is required.

Diagnostic Standards and Evaluation Techniques

Tools and Diagnostic Criteria for Schizoid Personality Disorder (SPD):

Mental health practitioners often use the criteria listed in the Diagnostic and Statistical Manual of Mental Disorders, Fifth Edition (DSM-5) to make a formal diagnosis of SPD. The following are the SPD diagnostic standards:

A. a widespread pattern of social withdrawal and a limited range of emotional expression in interpersonal situations that starts by early adulthood and manifests in several scenarios, as suggested by at least four of the following:

1. neither seeks nor values close bonds, including those with family.

2. selects solo activities almost always.

3. Possess little or no desire to engage in sexual activity with another individual.

4. enjoys very few, if any, activities.

5. outside of first-degree relatives, lacks close pals or confidants.

6. appears unconcerned with other people's compliments or criticism.

7. demonstrates emotion flatness, detachment, or coldness.

B. is not only a symptom of Schizophrenia, Bipolar Disorder, or Depressive Disorder and is not brought on by a substance (such as a drug of abuse or prescription) or a general medical condition's direct physiological consequences.

Assessment techniques: To determine whether a person has SPD, mental health practitioners may utilize a variety of assessment techniques and methodologies, such as:

1. Clinical interviews: in-depth discussions with the person to examine their background, behavior, and symptoms, as well as to rule out any potential mental health issues.

2. Clinical interviews that are structured and adhere to a predetermined set of questions and criteria can be used by mental health practitioners to determine whether SPD is present.

3. Self-Report Questionnaires: To learn more about a person's personality traits and life experiences, one can administer questionnaires and self-assessment instruments like the Schizoid Personality Questionnaire (SPQ).

4. Assessments based on observation: Observing a person's activities and interactions in a variety of social

settings can reveal important details about their interpersonal tendencies.

5. Collateral Information: Getting information from the person's friends, family, or other close friends might help us understand them more thoroughly, both socially and emotionally.

To distinguish SPD from other personality disorders or mental health diseases with comparable symptoms, the diagnosis of SPD requires a thorough evaluation by a licensed mental health practitioner. This procedure aids in the accurate diagnosis of the patient and the creation of a suitable treatment strategy.

Differential diagnosis and associated diseases

Schizoid Personality Disorder (SPD) Differential Diagnosis and Co-Occurring Conditions:

Differential diagnosis: Mental health providers must take into account other personality disorders and mental health illnesses that may present with comparable symptoms while evaluating a person for SPD. Differentiating SPD from these disorders is a component of differential diagnosis. The following conditions may be variably diagnosed with SPD:

1. People with avoidant personality disorder have a difficult time interacting with others, but their main concern is being rejected or criticized, which makes them extremely anxious in social settings. They want close relationships, unlike SPD, but steer clear of them out of anxiety.

2. Schizotypal Personality Disorder: Schizotypal Personality Disorder and SPD both exhibit quirky behavior and social withdrawal. However, Schizotypal PD patients may have bizarre beliefs and perceptual anomalies that are not SPD-specific.

3. Social Anxiety Disorder (Social Phobia): People with social anxiety disorder have a strong dread of being in public because they worry about being judged or

embarrassed. People with SPD often prefer isolation over social interactions rather than being afraid of them.

4. Autism Spectrum Disorders (ASD): Some characteristics of SPD, such as challenges in establishing strong connections and restricted emotional expression, may overlap with ASD. ASD, on the other hand, is a neurodevelopmental disease with a wider array of symptoms, such as difficulties with repetitive behavior and communication.

Co-Occurring Conditions: SPD sufferers may also have co-occurring mental health issues, which can make diagnosis and treatment more challenging. Co-occurring conditions with SPD include some of the following:

1. Depression: If a person with SPD becomes upset about their trouble developing relationships, social isolation and emotional detachment can worsen depressive symptoms.

2. Anxiety Disorders: People with SPD may also have concomitant anxiety disorders, such as phobias or generalized anxiety disorder, which are often socially related.

3. Substance Use Disorders: Some SPD sufferers may use drugs or alcohol to self-medicate their feelings of anxiety or sadness or to cope with the problems of their condition.

4. Other personality disorders: The clinical picture can become more complicated when other personality disorders, such as avoidant or schizotypal personality disorders, co-occur.

5. Post-Traumatic Stress Disorder (PTSD): Some people with SPD may develop PTSD as a result of traumatic events connected to social difficulties or rejection.

To identify any co-occurring illnesses and guarantee a thorough treatment plan that covers both SPD and any other potential mental health difficulties the individual may be experiencing, mental health practitioners must undertake a thorough examination.

CHAPTER 4

SPD Development and its Causes

Environmental and genetic influences

Schizoid Personality Disorder (SPD) Genetic and Environmental Contributors:

1. genetic influences

• Similar to other personality disorders, there is evidence to suggest that hereditary factors may contribute to the development of SPD. The personality traits and features associated with SPD may be influenced by particular genetic predispositions or vulnerabilities, according to some theories.

• According to family studies, those with a history of personality disorders, such as SPD, may be more likely to experience the condition themselves. However, particular genes or genetic markers linked to SPD have not yet been firmly identified.

2. environmental elements

• Early environmental exposures and parenting may also have an impact on SPD development. Some environmental elements that might be involved are as follows:

• Parental Attachment: An individual's capacity to develop deep relationships later in life can be impacted by early attachment experiences with caregivers. Emotional detachment in adulthood may be caused by a lack of solid bonding throughout childhood.

• Childhood Trauma: Childhood experiences of trauma, neglect, or abuse can cause emotional and social problems, which may help explain why SPD develops.

• Social Isolation: Growing up in circumstances devoid of social connection and interaction may reinforce a propensity for isolation and aid in the emergence of schizoid characteristics.

• Modeling Behavior: An individual's personal behavior and attitudes toward relationships can be influenced by observing and learning from family members or caregivers who display schizoid symptoms or patterns of social isolation.

It's crucial to remember that SPD, like other personality disorders, is probably the result of a complex interaction between genetic, environmental, and psychological variables. Not everyone who has a genetic tendency to SPD will experience it, and not all cases of SPD can be completely attributed to genetics or environmental factors. These elements must be taken into account to get a complete grasp of the disease. Early intervention as well as therapeutic assistance can help SPD sufferers control their symptoms and enhance their quality of life.

Earlier influences

Schizoid Personality Disorder (SPD) Childhood Inputs:

Schizoid Personality Disorder (SPD)-related personality traits and behavioral patterns can be greatly influenced by events and influences during childhood. The following childhood factors could have an impact on the emergence of SPD:

1. Parental interactions: Primary caregiver interactions, particularly those with parents, can have a significant impact. When their parents are emotionally unavailable, aloof, or inattentive, children may learn to repress their emotions and develop an emotional detachment tolerance.

2. Attachment Style: Early experiences of attachment with caregivers are essential for the growth of social and emotional abilities. Children who do not develop safe attachments may have trouble in their adult relationships with intimacy and trust.

3. Childhood trauma can cause emotional and psychological difficulties, such as physical or emotional

abuse, neglect, or witnessing violence. As a means of coping with the emotional anguish resulting from such situations, SPD may develop.

4. Growing up in a society where social isolation is the norm might reinforce a penchant for independence and solitary confinement. Children who grow up in dysfunctional or solitary families may exhibit SPD-like characteristics as a reaction to their environment.

5. Childhood friendships and interactions with peers also have an impact. Children who find it difficult to make lasting friendships or who feel rejected by their classmates may grow to prefer solitude and be afraid of social interaction.

6. Personality traits: Some people may be born with personality features that make them more prone to SPD. For instance, schizoid tendencies may be more likely to develop in adults who are introverted or highly independent as children.

It's crucial to keep in mind that not everyone who has a tough childhood goes on to develop SPD, and not everyone who has SPD has a rough childhood. Complex genetic, environmental, and psychological factors are likely contributing to the development of this personality disorder. Additionally, each person's personality development will be influenced differently by their childhood experiences. Individuals with SPD can address the effects of childhood influences and create healthy coping mechanisms for their emotions and social interactions with the aid of early intervention and treatment.

Issues with Attachment and Trauma

Schizoid Personality Disorder (SPD) and Attachment Disorder:

1. attachment issues: Early attachment experiences are crucial in the formation of personality traits and social behavior. About SPD:

• Insecure Attachment: People with SPD may have gone through periods of insecure attachment as infants or children. This implies that they might not have had constant emotional support and receptivity from their caretakers, which would make it challenging for them to establish secure and trusted connections in the future.

• Avoidant Attachment: Some SPD sufferers could adopt an avoidant attachment stance. They developed self-soothing skills and independence as a result of intermittent childcare during childhood. Their desire for seclusion and emotional detachment may result from this.

2. Trauma: Childhood or adult traumatic experiences might worsen or contribute to the development of SPD.

• Emotional Neglect: Children who have persistently had their emotional needs unfulfilled may learn to repress their emotions and develop a habit of emotional detachment as a coping mechanism.

• Abuse: Serious emotional and psychological problems can result from physical, emotional, or sexual abuse experienced as a child. Some people may exhibit symptoms resembling SPD as a coping method to shield themselves from further emotional suffering or vulnerability.

• Witnessing Violence: Childhood exposure to domestic violence or other traumatic experiences can also have an impact on an individual's emotional growth and may influence their tendency for emotional isolation and detachment.

CHAPTER 5

Having schizoid personality disorder and living

Problems with isolation

Schizoid Personality Disorder (SPD) Isolation Issues

1. Loneliness and Emotional Distress: Ironically, despite the fact that people with SPD may prefer solitude, they frequently feel incredibly lonely. Since they may want deep social ties yet struggle to make or keep them, this loneliness can cause mental pain.

2. Social isolation can be brought on by a propensity for solitude. With time, social support networks may become scarce as a result of this isolation, making it challenging for people with SPD to ask for assistance or company when they need it.

3. Relationship Difficulties: Avoiding social situations and expressing emotions rarely can make it difficult to build strong bonds. This might lead to the loss of chances for interpersonal growth, companionship, and emotional support.

4. Missed Life Experiences: Living alone means frequently losing out on social occasions, family get-togethers, and group activities. This may cause feelings of exclusion and the sensation that one is losing out on life's richness.

5. Limited Emotional Expression: People with SPD may become frustrated by their limited emotional expression and emotional detachment. They could struggle to express their emotions to others or to comprehend and manage the emotions of those around them.

6. Others may misunderstand or misinterpret people with SPD because they mistake their emotional

detachment for disinterest or apathy. Conflicts in society and increased isolation may result from this.

7. Challenges in the Workplace: In some situations, SPD features may have an impact on a person's career and workplace. The tendency toward solitary pursuits and little social interaction might affect teamwork and collaboration at work.

8. Risk of Depression and Anxiety: Loneliness, isolation, and restricted emotional expression all work together to raise the possibility that people with SPD will experience depression or anxiety disorders.

9. Difficulty Seeking Help: Due to their tendency for solitude and emotional detachment, people with SPD may have trouble getting help or participating in therapy. The process of getting help and support may be slowed down or prevented as a result.

It's critical to realize that while people with SPD may encounter these difficulties, they also possess skills and coping techniques that can support them as they navigate their particular circumstances. Treatment, such as counseling emphasizing social skill and emotional expression development, can offer helpful resources for addressing these issues and enhancing general wellbeing.

Interactions with others and relationships

Social Interactions and Relationships in Schizoid Personality Disorder (SPD):

1. Having Trouble Establishing Close Relationships: People with SPD frequently struggle to create and maintain close, personal relationships. Their emotional distance and inclination for solitude may make it difficult for them to build meaningful relationships with other people.

2. Limited Social Circle: People with SPD often have a small, trusted group of friends—if any—or no friends at

all. They could favor close relationships with a restricted group of people over more varied social interactions.

3. Social awkwardness: People with SPD may feel uncomfortable or awkward in social settings. They could find it difficult to strike up discussions, make small talk, or comprehend social signs and expectations.

4.Social Events Avoidance: Social events, parties, and gatherings may be shunned or reluctantly attended. Small conversations and shallow interactions are frequent in these scenarios, which people with SPD may find dull or anxiety-inducing.

5. Lack of Dating Interest: Many SPD sufferers show little interest in dating or committed relationships. They might not actively pursue romantic partners, and they might not feel romantic attraction in the same way that other people do.

6. Emotional Detachment: One of the main characteristics of SPD is emotional detachment, which

can make it challenging to emotionally connect with people. They could find it difficult to show affection or react to other people's emotional expressions.

7. Conflict avoidance: Because disagreements and conflicts in relationships may be emotionally upsetting for SPD individuals, they frequently avoid them. This avoidance might result in problems going unresolved and make it harder to resolve conflicts.

8. They frequently place a high emphasis on their independence and self-sufficiency. Relying on people or sharing responsibilities in relationships may become difficult as a result.

9. While solitude is preferred, it can also result in social isolation and fewer social support systems. This alone may lead to loneliness and a sensation of being misunderstood.

10. Desire for Understanding: Despite their social difficulties, people with SPD may want others'

acceptance. They could value relationships that provide them with a place to be themselves that is safe and judgment-free.

It's critical to understand that people with SPD can experience a variety of things in their relationships and social interactions. They could have difficulties, but they also have special talents and strengths. People with SPD can benefit from treatment and therapy to help them learn social skills, have a better understanding of emotions, and work toward more satisfying interpersonal and social connections.

A Work-Life Balance

For those who suffer from schizoid personality disorder (SPD), work and daily life are impacted.

1. Solitary Careers: Some SPD sufferers could be drawn to occupations that let them work alone and independently. It can be enticing to pursue a career in computer programming, writing, research, or some

forms of art because these fields offer independence and little opportunity for social connection.

2. Minimal Social Engagement at Work: People with SPD may favor jobs and tasks that require less social engagement. They might struggle with team projects, team meetings, or customer-facing jobs, but they might do well in jobs that don't involve much interaction with others.

3. Routine and predictability: People with SPD may prefer employment that is predictable and routine because they feel more in control and experience less social stress. They could be drawn to occupations that have simple processes and little surprises.

4. Challenges in Teamwork: People with SPD may experience difficulty in collaborative work settings and team-based tasks. They could have issues with teamwork requirements, communication, and group dynamics.

5. Job happiness for people with SPD frequently depends on how much autonomy, independence, and self-reliance their line of work permits. They might find fulfillment in occupations that allow them to focus on unique activities and projects.

6. Work-Life Balance: People with SPD may place more importance on their alone time and personal time outside of work. They frequently need to find a healthy work-life balance that allows them to have enough time for alone time and self-care.

7. Flexibility in the workplace: People with SPD may be able to adapt their employment choices due to their inclination for independence and solitude. They might be more willing to experiment with different employment options and adjust to unforeseen events.

8. Social Difficulties at Work: Despite their prowess in solitary pursuits, individuals could find it difficult to fit in at the office or have small conversations at networking

events. This may occasionally limit prospects for job progression.

9. Stress Management: People with SPD may turn to seclusion as a coping strategy. To refuel and decompress throughout the workweek, they could seek out little periods of isolation.

10. Conflict avoidance: People with SPD may be more likely to avoid conflict than to engage in it in difficult interpersonal or workplace settings. In the workplace, this strategy may offer advantages as well as drawbacks.

While those with SPD may experience some difficulties at work, it's crucial to remember that they also bring special strengths like self-sufficiency, attention to detail, and a great aptitude for autonomous work. Finding occupations that play to their talents and improve their general well-being can be facilitated by being aware of their requirements and preferences.

CHAPTER 6

Treatment and assistance

Therapeutic Methods

Schizoid Personality Disorder (SPD) Treatment Methods

1. The mainstay of SPD treatment is psychotherapy, sometimes known as talk therapy. There are many treatment modalities that can be helpful, including:

• Cognitive-Behavioral Therapy (CBT): CBT can assist people with SPD in recognizing and modifying harmful thought patterns and social interaction-related behaviors. Additionally, it can help with the development of better coping mechanisms and social skills.

• Psychodynamic Therapy: In psychodynamic therapy, unconscious mechanisms and early events that may be linked to SPD are examined. It can aid people in understanding their feelings and social tendencies.

• Schema therapy: The goal of schema therapy is to identify and treat core beliefs or faulty schemas. Addressing deeply rooted tendencies toward emotional detachment and avoidance can be very beneficial.

2. Group Therapy: In a safe, controlled environment, group therapy gives people with SPD the chance to hone social skills, make connections with others dealing with comparable issues, and receive feedback and support.

3. Social Skills Training: This kind of therapy aims to enhance social skills like starting conversations, keeping eye contact, and spotting social cues. It may be helpful for SPD sufferers who have trouble interacting with others.

4. Supportive Therapy: Supportive therapy helps people with SPD feel understood and accepted by providing emotional support and validation. It might offer a secure setting for them to process their feelings and encounters.

5. Meditation and mindfulness practices can help people with SPD become more conscious of their feelings and thoughts, which can help them control their emotional reactivity and maintain their composure in social situations.

6.Medication: While not the main course of therapy for SPD, medication may be taken into consideration in situations where co-occurring disorders like depression or anxiety are present. The symptoms of these co-occurring illnesses can be reduced with medication.

7. Occupational therapy: Occupational therapy can help people with SPD create and maintain routines, enhance everyday functioning, and discover enjoyable activities to do alone.

8. Self-Help Techniques: Supporting people with SPD in the development of self-help techniques, such as making minor social objectives or establishing routines, can give them the capacity to transform their lives for the better.

9. In some circumstances, including family members in therapy can be helpful, especially when family dynamics influence or contribute to the symptoms of SPD.

10. Long-Term Support: To address their particular issues and continue their personal progress, many SPD sufferers benefit from continued counseling and support.

CHAPTER 7

Embracing Uniqueness and Discovering Meaning

Drugs and complementary therapies

Schizoid Personality Disorder (SPD) Medication and Alternative Therapies:

1. Medicine: Since SPD is thought of as a personality disorder rather than a mental condition that responds well to medication, medication is typically not the main treatment for SPD itself. However, a mental health practitioner may recommend medication to treat the symptoms of SPD in people who also have co-occurring diseases, including anxiety, depression, or other mood disorders. Typical drugs prescribed include:

• Antidepressants: To treat the sadness and anxiety symptoms that frequently co-occur with SPD, selective serotonin reuptake inhibitors (SSRIs) or other antidepressants may be administered.

• Anti-Anxiety Drugs: Anti-anxiety drugs may be recommended on a short-term basis to treat distress in cases of severe anxiety or panic symptoms.

2. Alternative Therapies and Self-Help Techniques: Although there isn't a single alternative therapy created specifically for SPD, SPD sufferers can investigate a variety of self-help techniques and complementary therapies that support health and personal development. These may consist of:

• Mindfulness and meditation: Mindfulness techniques can assist people with SPD in being more conscious of their emotions and thinking processes, which can enhance emotional regulation and self-awareness.

• Yoga: Yoga incorporates breathing exercises, physical postures, and meditation methods. It may be an effective technique for easing tension and encouraging serenity.

• Painting and Creative Therapies: Using your creativity in painting, music, or writing can be helpful and give you a way to express yourself.

• Physical activity: Regular exercise can improve mood and general well-being. It may also present chances for introspection and seclusion.

• Self-Help Books and Resources: People with SPD may benefit from reading self-help books and online resources about social skills, self-improvement, and personal growth.

• Regular Routines: Setting up regular daily routines can help people with SPD manage their time well and keep their lives feeling organized and in control.

3. Diet and lifestyle: Leading a healthy lifestyle that includes a balanced diet, frequent exercise, and enough

sleep can help people feel better overall and control their emotions.

4. Support Groups: Participating in support groups, whether in person or online, can give SPD sufferers a forum to interact with others going through similar struggles, share stories, and ask for help.

5. Therapeutic Writing: Journaling or therapeutic writing exercises can assist people with SPD in exploring their feelings, ideas, and unique insights.

It's important to keep in mind that different people may respond differently to alternative therapies and self-help techniques. The optimal solution will vary depending on personal tastes and requirements. For people who have SPD, therapy, self-care techniques, and, if required, medication can all help enhance health and quality of life. The best treatment strategy can be chosen with the assistance of a mental health expert.

Constructing a Support System

The Development of a Support Network for People with Schizoid Personality Disorder (SPD):

1. Encourage the SPD patient to seek therapy from a licensed mental health practitioner with knowledge of treating personality disorders. They can work on personal development, social skills development, and emotion exploration in therapy.

2. Educate relatives and friends: To better their awareness of SPD, educate close relatives and friends about the disorder. This can facilitate better communication and lessen misunderstandings.

3. Supportive Friends and Family: Encourage people with SPD to keep in touch with understanding and supportive friends and family. These people can provide company and emotional support.

4. Joining support groups for people with personality disorders or those that are SPD-specific is advised. These

organizations can give people a feeling of acceptance, affirmation, and the chance to share their experiences.

5. Online Communities: SPD-specific forums and communities can be helpful resources for knowledge and support. Even if they favor online encounters, they enable people to connect with others who have comparable experiences.

6. Set Reasonable Expectations: Encourage people with SPD to tell their support network what they need and desire. Relationships can be enhanced and stress reduced by having reasonable expectations for social interactions and emotional expression.

7. Social Skills Training: If the patient is willing, social skills training can be incorporated into their therapy. These abilities may aid them in navigating social situations more successfully.

8. Empathy and Patience: When engaging with someone who has SPD, family members and friends should

demonstrate empathy and patience. Recognize that their lack of feeling is not a sign of rejection but rather a feature of their condition.

9. Respecting Boundaries: It's important to acknowledge each person's demand for privacy and personal space. Don't force children into social situations they find awkward, and give them the freedom to establish their own boundaries.

10. Encourage Self-Care: Assist people with SPD in their self-care practices and wellness-enhancing activities. These can include participating in solo hobbies, working out, meditating, or other satisfying pursuits.

11. Maintaining regular check-ins will allow you to determine whether they require any further support and how they are feeling emotionally. Pay attention to any adjustments in their conduct or attitude.

12. Professional Support for the Family: If family dynamics play a role in the difficulties the SPD patient

faces, family therapy or counseling may be an option to address any underlying problems and enhance communication.

Creating a support network for people with SPD can greatly improve their emotional health and quality of life. It's critical to approach this process with tolerance, cognizance, and a readiness to adjust to their particular requirements and preferences.

Techniques for Personal Development

Schizoid Personality Disorder (SPD) Patients' Personal Growth Strategies

1. Engage in counseling with a mental health expert who specializes in personality problems and conduct self-examination exercises. Utilize therapy as a setting for self-discovery, emotional awareness, and coping skill development.

2. Emotional Awareness and Mindfulness: Use mindfulness practices to increase your awareness of

your thoughts and emotions. This can enhance emotional control and help you comprehend your inner world better.

3. Consider social skills training if you're receptive to it to improve your ability to negotiate social situations, form connections, and form relationships.

4. Setting Achievable Social Goals: To venture beyond your comfort zone, gradually set tiny, doable social goals. For instance, spend a little time at a social gathering, strike up a conversation with a coworker, or sign up for a club or group that shares your interests.

5. Create daily habits that allow you to spend both time alone and time interacting with others. You can retain stability and interact with others in a controllable way with the aid of this equilibrium.

6. Prioritize self-care routines like regular exercise, a healthy diet, getting enough sleep, and stress-reduction techniques like yoga or meditation.

7. Journaling: Write your ideas, emotions, and experiences down in a journal. You can track your personal development and acquire insights into your emotions by keeping a journal.

8. Explore Your Interests: Keep pursuing lonely pastimes and pursuits that make you happy and complete. These pursuits may provide one with a sense of fulfillment and purpose.

9. Explore writing exercises for therapeutic purposes to better express your feelings and think through issues.

10. Don't be afraid to ask friends, family, or support groups for assistance. Talk about your struggles and experiences with sympathetic and understanding people.

11. Read and learn more about personality disorders, SPD, and general mental health. You can better manage your condition if you have a better understanding of it.

12. Acceptance and self-compassion: Exercise acceptance and self-compassion. Recognize that SPD is a part of who you are and that it's acceptable to have special preferences and difficulty interacting with others.

13. Set Achievable Goals: For personal development, set realistic goals. Be kind to yourself and acknowledge your progress, no matter how minor.

14. Professional Assistance: Persist in working with a mental health specialist to address particular difficulties and chart your path toward personal development.

Every person's journey to personal growth is different, and it happens gradually. Respect your desire for solitude and self-care while also being nice to yourself and realizing that development can require stepping outside of your comfort zone.

Developing passion and creativity

Developing Passion and Creativity for People with Schizoid Personality Disorder (SPD):

1. Investigate Your Creative Outlets: Take part in creative endeavors that fit with your talents and interests. Creativity may be a meaningful and solitary method to channel your passion, whether it be through writing, music, painting, or any other type of artistic expression.

2. Create personal projects: Get started on exciting personal projects. These initiatives might provide people with a sense of direction and inspiration. To feel accomplished, divide the chores into smaller, more doable ones.

3. Solitary Activities: Make the most of your inclination to be alone by using it to explore your interests in more depth. The best places for creativity and self-expression are frequently found in solitary pursuits.

4. Explore books, articles, or online courses that are relevant to your interests while you read and learn. Learning new topics can spark interest and provide inspiration for new creative endeavors.

5. Create a Space for Creativity: Set aside a physical area in your home where you can engage in creative activities. The presence of a dedicated space can improve motivation and focus.

6. Obtaining Inspiration: Look for inspiration from a variety of sources, including personal experiences, literature, art, and nature. These resources can stoke your passion and creativity.

7. Establish objectives for your creative endeavors. Setting goals and benchmarks can give you focus and a sense of accomplishment.

8. When you're ready, collaborate. Even though you might prefer to work alone, think about working with people who have similar interests. Collaborative

ventures can present fresh viewpoints and development opportunities.

9. Embrace mindful creativity by staying present while working on your projects. Being in the moment can improve your creative process and help you connect more deeply with your passion.

10. Don't be scared to explore and attempt new things when it comes to your artistic endeavors. Innovation frequently results in rekindled enthusiasm and passion.

11. When you feel comfortable, share your creations with dependable friends or online communities. Receiving encouraging comments and inspiring others can be fulfilling.

12. Make sure to strike a good balance between your creative endeavors and your self-care. Make self-care a top priority if you want to avoid burnout and keep your love for your activities alive.

Even if you have SPD, developing your creativity and passion can make your life happier and more fulfilling. Accept your distinct viewpoint and tastes, and let them direct you on an authentically you-aligned creative journey.

Stories of achievement and motivational journeys

Schizoid personality disorder (SPD) sufferers' inspirational journeys and success stories serve as models of resilience and personal development. Even though SPD has its own set of difficulties, many people have managed to thrive and lead happy, fulfilled lives. The following are some motivating elements of their journeys:

1. Self-Awareness and Self-Acceptance: Many SPD sufferers have recounted their experiences with self-knowledge and self-acceptance. They have gained a better understanding of their personality traits and

preferences through therapy and introspection, which has increased self-acceptance and self-compassion.

2. Passion and Creativity: Some SPD sufferers have used their inclination for seclusion to fuel their artistic endeavors. They have found success and notoriety in pursuits like literature, art, music, and research since these are their areas of passion.

3. Academic and professional success: Despite social difficulties, some SPD sufferers have achieved academic and professional success. They have been able to make substantial contributions in their chosen disciplines because of their laser-like focus and attention to detail in their work.

4. Building Support Systems: Many people have succeeded in constructing networks of sympathetic friends and family members. These ties and partnerships offer emotional support, proving that people with SPD can also create deep bonds.

5. Advocates for mental health awareness: Some SPD sufferers have taken on this role, sharing their stories to dispel stigma and inform others about personality disorders. They have helped society understand SPD better as a result of their efforts.

6. Personal Development: Inspirational journeys frequently require developing personally and getting through social obstacles. People with SPD have talked about gradually stepping outside of their social comfort zones and making deep connections.

7. Therapeutic Success Stories: Success stories typically highlight therapeutic success. Individuals with SPD have improved their social skills, established coping mechanisms, and improved their emotional wellbeing under the direction of mental health specialists.

8. Finding Purpose: Through meaningful employment, advocacy, or close relationships, many people have

discovered a sense of purpose in life. For those with SPD, purpose can be a strong motivator.

These motivational tales show that having SPD does not prevent one from achieving success, happiness, or personal growth. People with SPD can find their abilities, interests, and ways to interact with others, which will ultimately result in a more fulfilling life journey, even though the path may have its own special hurdles.

Printed in Great Britain
by Amazon

40039842R00046